I0437755

Make Your Own Book No. 2
50 Elaborate Oval Frames for Coloring

Coloring Books by Alberta Hutchinson

Home Made Books Coloring Books, available from www.createspace.com, and major booksellers:

Sacred Design Series:

Make Your Own Book No. 1 — 50 Elaborate Round Frames for Coloring, with Text Lines
Available at www.createspace.com/4704942

Make Your Own Book No. 2 — 50 Elaborate Oval Frames for Coloring
Available at www.createspace.com/4765016

Mandala Designs Coloring Book No. 1 — 35 New Mandala Designs
Available at www.createspace.com/4506373

Mandala Designs Coloring Book No. 2 — 32 New Mandala Designs
Available at www.createspace.com/4555976

Mandala Designs Coloring Book No. 3 — 32 New Mandala Designs
Available at www.createspace.com/4614672

Fantasy Flowers Coloring Book No. 1 — 24 Designs in Elaborate Oval Frames
Available at www.createspace.com/4446137

Fantasy Flowers Coloring Book No. 2 — 32 Designs in an Elaborate Square Frame
Available at www.createspace.com/4485357

Snowflake Designs Coloring Book — 24 Designs in Elaborate Frames
Available at www.createspace.com/4446148

Dover Publications Coloring Books by Alberta Hutchinson, available from major booksellers:

Mystical Mandala Coloring Book

Infinite Coloring Mandala Design CD and Book, by Martha Bartfeld and Alberta Hutchinson

Square Mandalas

Lotus Designs

Creative Haven Lotus Designs Coloring Book (Creative Haven Coloring Books), by Alberta Hutchinson and Creative Haven

3-D Coloring Book — Mandalas, by Martha Bartfeld and Alberta Hutchinson

MAKE YOUR OWN BOOK

- by -

Alberta Hutchinson

2

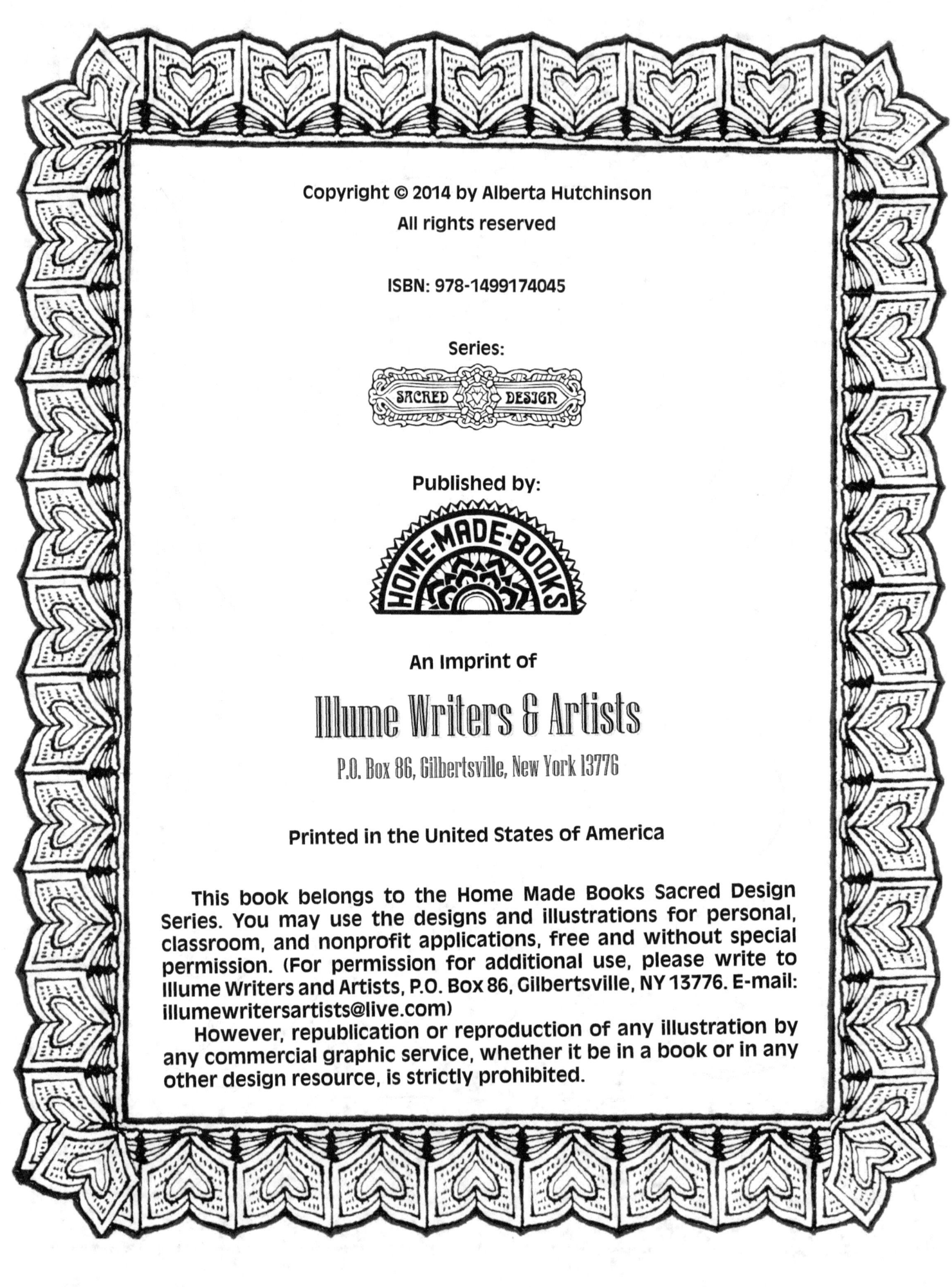

Copyright © 2014 by Alberta Hutchinson

All rights reserved

ISBN: 978-1499174045

Series:

SACRED DESIGN

Published by:

HOME-MADE-BOOKS

An Imprint of

Illume Writers & Artists

P.O. Box 86, Gilbertsville, New York 13776

Printed in the United States of America

This book belongs to the Home Made Books Sacred Design Series. You may use the designs and illustrations for personal, classroom, and nonprofit applications, free and without special permission. (For permission for additional use, please write to Illume Writers and Artists, P.O. Box 86, Gilbertsville, NY 13776. E-mail: illumewritersartists@live.com)

However, republication or reproduction of any illustration by any commercial graphic service, whether it be in a book or in any other design resource, is strictly prohibited.

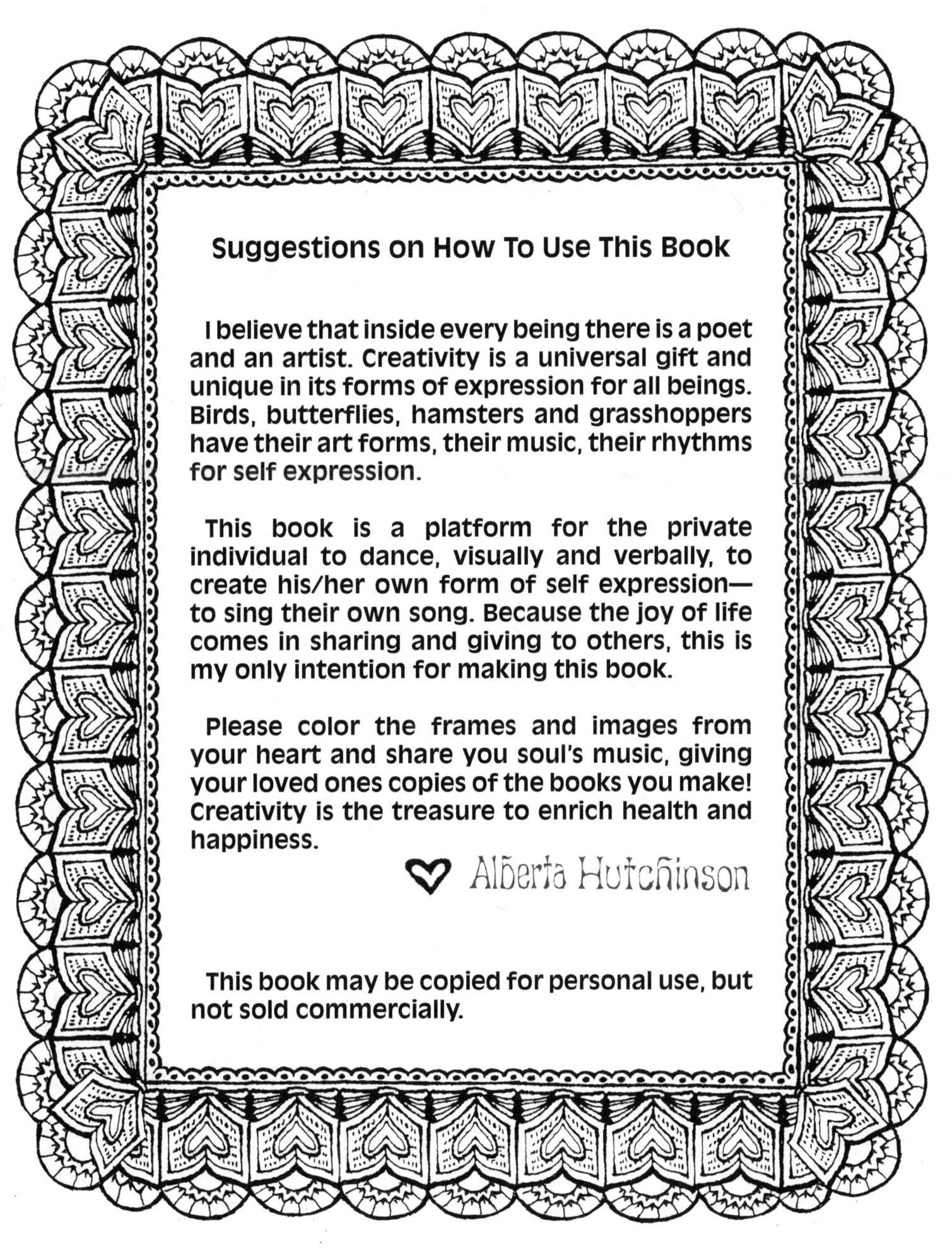

Suggestions on How To Use This Book

I believe that inside every being there is a poet and an artist. Creativity is a universal gift and unique in its forms of expression for all beings. Birds, butterflies, hamsters and grasshoppers have their art forms, their music, their rhythms for self expression.

This book is a platform for the private individual to dance, visually and verbally, to create his/her own form of self expression— to sing their own song. Because the joy of life comes in sharing and giving to others, this is my only intention for making this book.

Please color the frames and images from your heart and share you soul's music, giving your loved ones copies of the books you make! Creativity is the treasure to enrich health and happiness.

♥ Alberta Hutchinson

This book may be copied for personal use, but not sold commercially.

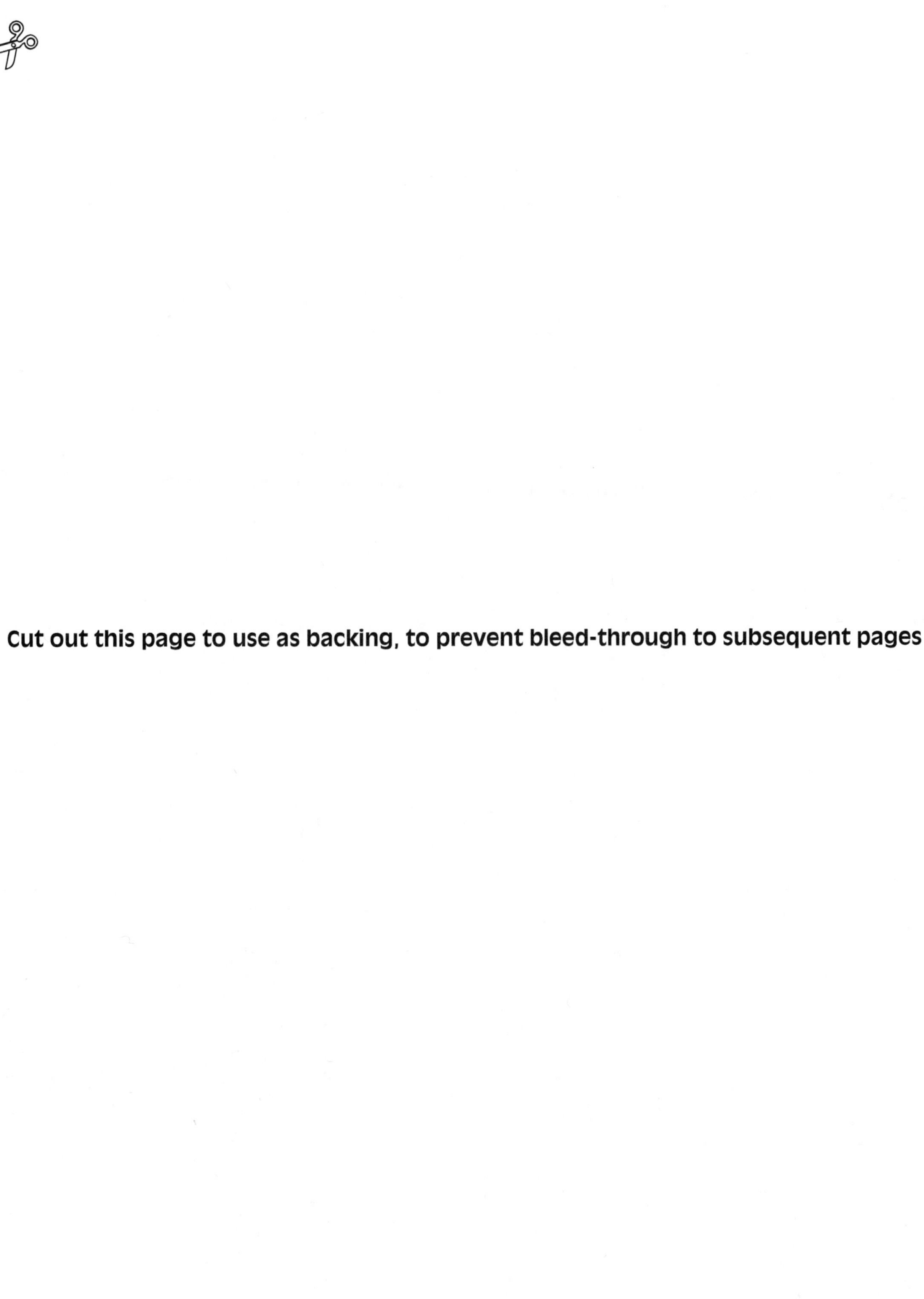

Cut out this page to use as backing, to prevent bleed-through to subsequent pages

2

11

12

19

25

41

44

45

48

www.ingramcontent.com/pod-product-compliance
Lightning Source LLC
Chambersburg PA
CBHW052003280526
45793CB00005B/828